W9-BJB-305

621.3   Oleksy, Walter G.
OLE
            Lasers.

DISCARDED

$15.27   33197000018478

DATE			
3-8			

BAKER & TAYLOR BOOKS

A New True Book

LASERS

By Walter Oleksy

CHILDRENS PRESS ®

CHICAGO

Laser beam demonstration at the
Toronto Science Museum

Library of Congress Cataloging-in-Publication Data

Oleksy, Walter G., 1930-
    Lasers.

    (A New true book)
    Includes index.
    Summary: Discusses the many uses of lasers in
science, industry, health, space, optics, video, and
almost every imaginable part of our lives.
    1. Lasers—Juvenile literature. [1. Lasers]
I. Title.
TA1682.044   1986   621.36'6   85-30894
ISBN 0-516-01282-7   AACR2

PHOTO CREDITS

Batelle's Columbus Division—17

Cameramann International, Ltd.—21
(right), 23, 40 (2 photos)

Cincinnati Milacron—43 (bottom
right)

Coherent General—43 (top and
bottom left)

Tony Freeman Photographs—37

Hewlett Packard—7 (bottom right)

Hughes Aircraft Company—9, 34

Journalism Services:
©Paul E. Burd—25 (top)
Journalism Services/SIU—7 (top), 25
(bottom)

Museum of the Fine Arts Research
and Holographic Center, Chicago:
©R. Flanagan/Image Finders—31
(2 photos), 33 (left)

Nawrocki Stock Photo:
© Candee Productions—38 (top)
© Ken Love— 10 (bottom), 19
© Wm. S. Nawrocki—2, 4 (top)
© Ken Sexton—21 (left)
© Carlos Vergara—cover, 10 (top)

Photri—28

Nuclear Division, Union Carbide
Corporation—44

University of California, Lawrence
Livermore National Laboratory and
Department of Energy—26

© Robert Walsh—12 (right)

Wide World—4 (bottom), 7 (bottom
left), 13, 15, 32, 35, 36, 38 (bottom)

© Jerome Wyckoff—12 (left)

Cover: Laser demonstration allows
        students to see how lasers
        work

TABLE OF CONTENTS

Powerful laser beams (above) are used as cutting tools.
In *Star Wars* Luke Skywalker (below left) fought with a "laser-light sword."

LASERS–
THE MIRACLE LIGHT

In the movie *Star Wars,* Luke Skywalker and Darth Vader fought with "laser-light swords." Laser swords don't exist, but lasers do.

Lasers are very powerful, accurate beams of light. They can be used for many things.

Doctors use lasers in operations instead of surgical knives.

Lasers track volcanic gases. They also measure winds in storms.

In computers and communications, lasers carry thousands of times more information than electrical signals carry.

Lasers create holograms—three-dimensional images.

Lasers weld car parts together and cut teeth in saws. They guide

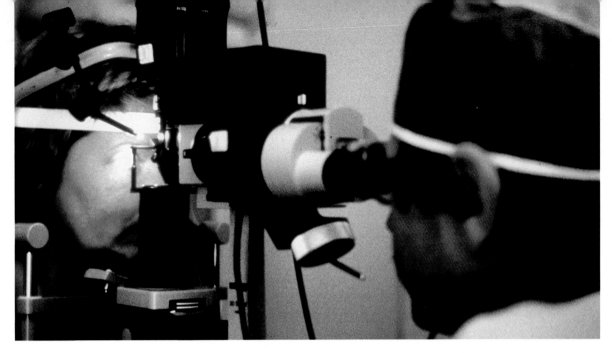

Doctor (above) performs eye surgery using a laser beam. The color
laser scanner (below left) is used to separate color photographs
into four components—blue, red, yellow, and black. The film
made by the laser scanner will be used to make plates for the printing
press. Laser beams are used to print type onto paper (below-right).

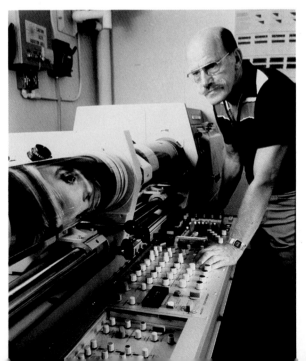

equipment in cutting tunnels and laying roads.

Lasers already are being used in space shuttle missions.

Scientists predict this is just the start of a "laser revolution" that will change our lives in many more ways.

Laser demonstration (above) allows students to see how lasers work. Surgeon (right) adjusts a laser used in surgery.

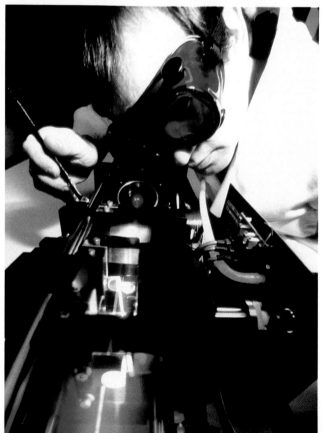

WHAT LASERS ARE AND HOW THEY BEGAN

The word *laser* is made up of the first letters of the words that describe it: *light amplification* by *stimulated emission* of *radiation*—laser.

Lasers are a device for the creation, amplification, and transmission of a narrow, intense beam of coherent light.

Ordinary light, such as sunlight and candlelight, spreads out. Laser beams do not. They can be focused in a single direction.

There are two kinds of light: ordinary and coherent.

Ordinary light is the light from the sun, a light bulb, or a fire. It contains many different wavelengths that are out of step with each other.

Coherent light is made

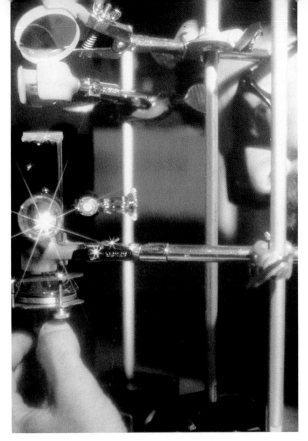

A Los Alamos National Laboratory physicist aligns a sample that will be examined by a laser detection system. Laser beams are used to study the elements found in material, such as coal dust.

up of waves of the same length. They are all in step with each other.

Most lasers produce an intense light. Some are tiny as a pinhead. Others are large as a football field.

Lasers can keep their size, direction, and strength over very long distances.

Ordinary light, on the other hand, spreads out and weakens, like the light from a flashlight.

Some laser beams shoot out in pulses lasting a fraction of a second. Others can beam on steadily for years.

Albert Einstein thought about lasers in 1917. He thought that atoms or

In 1964
Dr. Theodore H.
Maiman
demonstrated one
of his laser
experiments.

molecules could, under certain conditions, absorb light or other radiation. If they could be stimulated or "pushed," they could give off their borrowed energy.

An American physicist, Theodore H. Maiman, created the first operating laser in 1960.

Maiman captured the glare of a flash lamp in a rod of a man-made ruby. It produced short, intense bursts of red light. They were so brilliant, they outshone the sun.

Some people fear lasers as "death-ray" weapons. But many scientists predict that lasers will be used as weapons only in science fiction. They foresee widespread use of lasers for peaceful purposes.

LASERS IN SCIENCE AND INDUSTRY

Lasers direct intense light with great accuracy and penetrating ability. They can cut or weld delicate electronic circuits or heavy metal parts such

This carbon-dioxide laser and advanced computer system is used to develop improved, low-cost technology for such common assembly line work as welding and cutting.

as those used to build automobiles or jet planes.

Lasers can melt the surface of a piece of steel so quickly that the metal will remain cool.

Laser energy can be "pulsed," or delivered in short bursts. These pulses make it possible to control physical and chemical

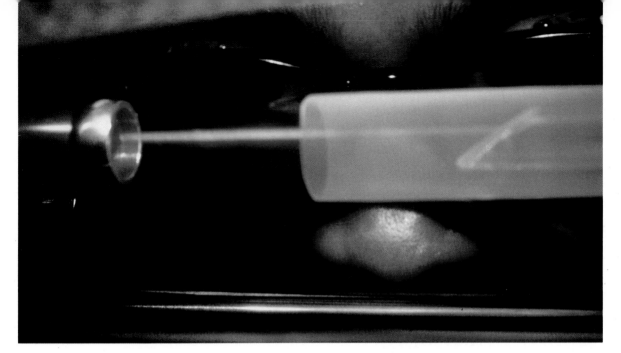

Close-up of a pulsed laser beam

processes in time as well as in space and energy. Lasers help reveal things scientists could never before see, make, or measure.

Lasers' extreme accuracy make them very useful as

a surveyor's tool. Tunnels can be drilled and roads laid very accurately with the use of laser-guided machines.

Lasers helped develop a new, high-power electrical switch. A pulse of laser light activates the device. It turns on electricity in less than a billionth of a second.

Lasers are used in the supermarket. The bars and stripes on almost every item in the store are

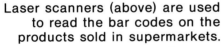

Laser scanners (above) are used
to read the bar codes on the
products sold in supermarkets.

scanned by a laser linked
to a computer. They
identify the product and
tell the checkout register
its price.

Lasers will be used
more and more in science
and industry in the future.

LASERS IN HEALTH AND MEDICINE

Lasers were first used for medical purposes in 1961. Now they have become routine for many surgical operations.

Laser energy offers more precise, cleaner cutting than the knife or scalpel.

Laser light beams can burn up unhealthy cells one at a time and sterilize

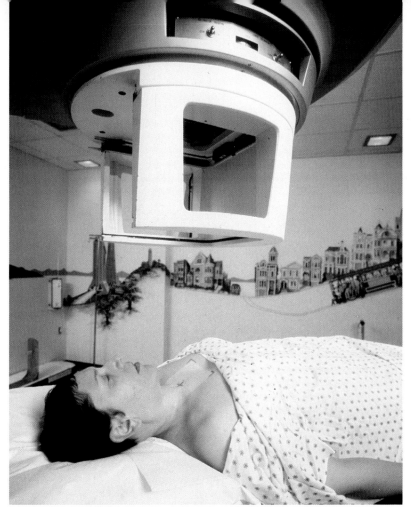

Red lines on the patient's chest mark the area that will receive radiation. Lasers are so precise that they can direct the radiation to only the spot that needs it, and, therefore, reduce damage to healthy cells.

the wound all at the same time.

Argon lasers are being used to "melt" tissue, mend blood vessels and

23

nerves. Other laser light is used to reach deep-seated tumors of the brain.

Lasers are used in eye, skin, and genital-tract surgery, in cancer treatment, and now in coronary (heart) surgery.

Lasers also are helping thousands of women who were unable to have children. Laser surgery can repair damaged internal

Cancer patient (above) sits in front of a neutron tunnel
chamber. The alignment of his body was determined by laser beams.
Close-up of the powerful laser beam (below) used in eye surgery.

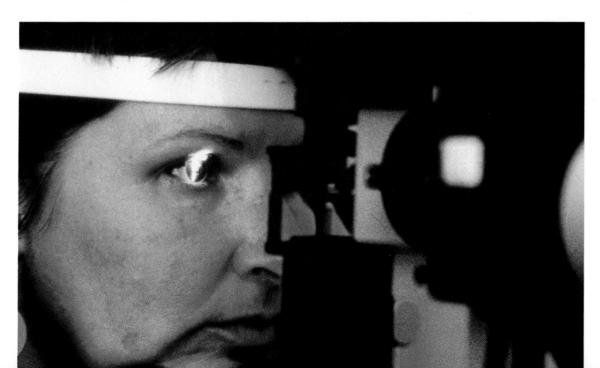

This Nova target chamber, built for research purposes, is the most powerful and flexible laser to date. Each of the five blue chambers directs a laser beam on a single spot inside the chamber.

organs, making childbearing possible.

Scientists are close to creating an X-ray laser. It could allow doctors to see three-dimensional pictures of the workings of the human body.

LASERS AND ENERGY

A pulsed laser beam can deliver a trillion watts of power. That's as much electric power as is being used over the entire earth at any one time.

Each year, high-energy lasers are bringing scientists closer to harnessing the energy source of the stars— nuclear fusion.

Laser fusion is producing nuclear energy by heating, crushing, and fusing hydrogen isotopes with laser light. This could solve the world's energy problems.

Some scientists think that it will be possible to build satellites that would be capable of shooting down enemy rockets with laser beams.

LASERS AND "STAR WARS" TECHNOLOGY

Scientists are trying to develop laser and other technology that could be used in America's "Star Wars" defense program.

An X-ray laser antimissile space weapon is being developed which could be powered by a nuclear bomb. It is called Super Excalibur, after the legend of the sword that King Arthur pulled from a stone.

The nuclear X-ray laser would take the power of a nuclear explosion and channel it into laser rods. These would give off powerful bursts of radiation. The energy of the laser pulse could shatter a missile with incredible force.

HOLOGRAPHY
AND LASER OPTICS
AND GRAPHICS

You may have seen covers of magazines that seem to jump out at you, like a 3-D movie off a

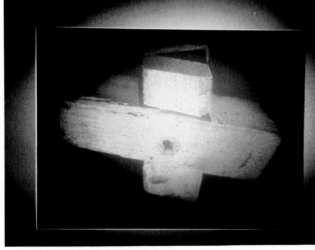

"Spider" hologram (left) and "Sawed Horse" hologram (above), displayed at the Museum of Holography in Chicago, Illinois

Dennis Gabor won the 1971 Nobel Prize in physics for his invention of holography.

screen. That's holography—three-dimensional laser photography.

A Hungarian, Dennis Gabor, invented holography in 1947. It is a way to take pictures without camera lenses.

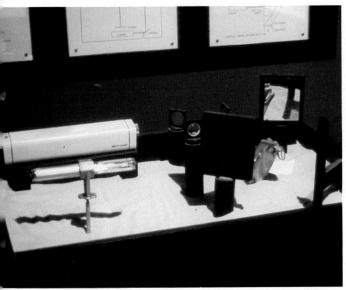

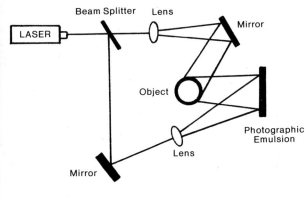

Holography equipment (left) and a diagram (right), showing how the laser beam interacts with the lenses and mirrors to create a hologram

Holography works with light, sound, or electron waves. A holograph of an object is made by using a laser light source and a system of mirrors and lenses.

U.S. Marine demonstrates a laser called Mule Modular Universal Laser Equipment. It will "Light the Way" and allow forward observers to set target distances for laser-guided weapons and conventional artillery.

There are many uses for holography. It inspects car and airplane parts in factories. It scans grocery product codes at supermarkets. It guides pilots with 3-D laser-radar.

Holography and computerized lasers are

The Last Starfighter was loaded with special effects that were created by laser beams and holography.

creating amazing special effects in movies such as *The Last Starfighter.* Exciting space battles are created by holography and lasers instead of models that take more time and are more expensive to build.

A piece of string is used to interrupt the almost invisible laser beam from a generator (at right). As the laser beam hit the string this brilliant starburst was created.

X-ray holograms will allow scientists to study in detail objects as small as viruses and DNA (life-force) molecules.

Also ahead could be 3-D movies on television.

Laser music disc

LASERS IN VIDEO AND AUDIO

Laser video discs and players are producing incredibly clear movies for home viewing. The pictures are far better than even

Congressman Jack F. Kemp (below left) examines a video
system that can be hooked up to any television set and
operated by inserting a single laser video disc.

the best videotape
recording, and carry full
stereo sound.

Compact audio discs
and players combine laser
and digital technology for
the best sound yet for
music fans.

At the same time, CDs
(compact discs) resist
scratches, dust, and normal
tracking wear of
conventional phonograph
records.

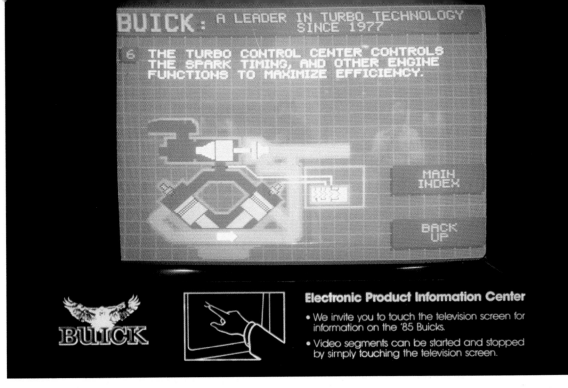

Computerized display (above) for Buick combines computer systems
with laser optical video discs. The Apple MacIntosh computer
(below) has a laser optical scanner that enables it to read and
display on the screen verbal or graphic documents.

Laser video discs are made by focusing a precise light beam onto a reflective surface dotted with billions of microscopic holes. These are encoded with visual or audio music, the contents of an art museum, or an entire encyclopedia.

Tomorrow's books may be printed on laser discs.

LASERS AND THE FUTURE

The future of laser technology is almost unlimited.

Laser-operated robots will work in the factory of the future.

Lasers will provide better satellite-to-satellite communications.

The robot arm (above) uses a laser beam to cut or weld. The laser system (below left) is designed to cut patterns. Lasers and computers allow the robot (right) to build other robots.

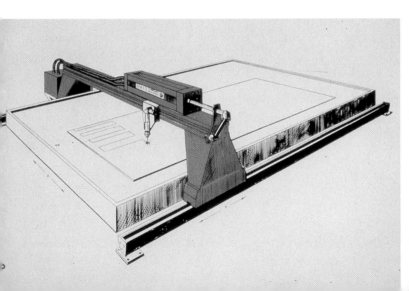

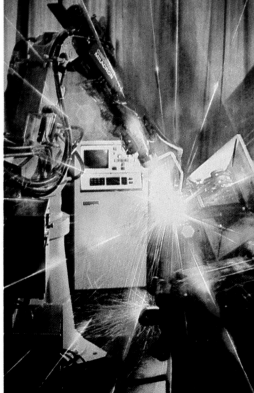

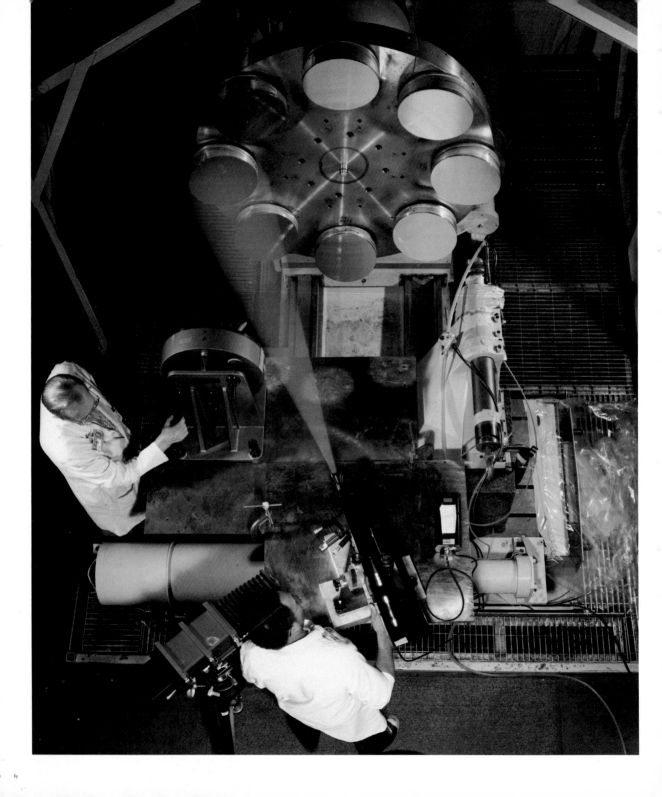

Lasers promise to help scientists develop fusion power, which could solve the world's energy problems. If power plants are built in space, their energy probably will be beamed down to the earth by laser.

Laser technology already borders on the miraculous. Scientists predict the best is yet to come.

Opposite page:
Technicians use a laser meter to inspect the surface finish of metal mirrors that were built for laser experiments. The mirrors were finished to an accuracy of a few millionths of an inch as determined by the laser measuring device.

WORDS YOU SHOULD KNOW

amplification(am • ple • fe • KA • shun) — an increase in strength, made louder or brighter

beam(BEEM) — a ray or shaft of light

coherent light(ko • HEAR • ant) — consistent light, light made up of waves of the same wavelength

electron(i • LEK • tron) — a particle of matter

energy(EN • er • jee) — the ability to do work; power

fusion(FYOO • zhen) — merging together; uniting atomic nuclei to release tremendous energy

hologram(HO • luh • gram) — a three-dimensional picture

image(IM • ij) — a likeness or picture of a person or object

isotopes(EYE • so • topes) — species of atoms

laser(LAY • zer) — a very powerful, accurate beam of light

missile(MIS • el) — a space weapon such as a rocket

molecule(MOL • e • kyul) — particle of matter

ordinary light(ORD • n • er • ee) — common light, such as from the sun or a light bulb

pulsed(PULST) — stimulated; a brief increase in current or voltage

radiation(ray • dee • A • shun) — the process whereby energy is emitted as particles or waves

robot(RO • bot) — a machine that functions on command

satellite(SAT • e • light) — an object that revolves around a planet

X-ray(EKS RAY) — a form of electromagnetic radiation

INDEX

About the Author

Walter Oleksy lives in Evanston, Illinois. He is a freelance writer and has published many articles and books for the juvenile and adult market.